MW01180595

The Lion in the Wheelchair
1st Edition
by
Michael Carr

©2018 Lulu Author. All rights reserved.
ISBN 978-0-359-12171-7

ACKNOWLEDGMENTS

I would like to thank my many friends, who supported me in the writing of this book. I could not say enough about my industrious wife, Deborah Carr, who typed and edited this book. A special thanks goes to Kris Zink for her prodigious typing and associate editor responsibilities. Milena Jackson worked on the design and cover for this book as well as searching ways to publish this book. This book would not have been published without her vision and persistence. I would also like to thank Thomas Weil, Chris Ford, Erik Jackson, Rina Karle, Taryn Hunter, and Joy Visavachaipan Stoops for contributing all the beautiful images for my manuscript.

Thank you to all who prayed and encouraged me during my time writing this book, "The Lion In The Wheelchair."

— Michael Carr

Isaiah 61: 1-3

The spirit of the Lord God is upon me,
because the Lord has anointed me;
He has sent me to bring good news to the afflicted,
to bind up the brokenhearted,
To proclaim liberty to the captives,
release to the prisoners,
To announce a year of favor from the Lord
and a day of vindication by our God;
To comfort all who mourn;
to place on those who mourn in Zion
a diadem instead of ashes,
To give them oil of gladness instead of mourning,
a glorious mantle instead of a faint spirit.

TABLE OF CONTENTS

1. The Lion In The Wheelchair

4. Will You Pray With Me?

6. A Humble Soul

7. Sustained By God

9. The Gift

12. The House of Self

13. What Will Become Of Me?

16. Who Am I?

17. Humble Man

20. Time

21. The Mud Puddle

23. Friends

26. Telephone Number & Address

27. Tenderly

29. Because of Me

31. Message from the Baby

34. The Drum

35. Focus

38. The Cross

39. Watchmen

42. Have You Ever Wrestled With Evil?

44. The Echo

46. I Was Weak

47. The Key to My Kingdom

50. Children, A Parable

52. The Meal

53. Gift Of Work

56. The Mask

57. Victory

61. A Tribute

63. The Garden

66. Rescue

68. The Aching Heart

70. On Target

72. The Promise

73. The Adversary

76. Perseverance

77. I AM

79. I Know How You Feel

81. The Dance of Heaven

84. Parched

85. Mighty to Save

87. I Need You

89. How to Love

92. A Fist Full Of Blessings

94. Humility

96. Accomplishments

97. Wrestling

100. Sweet Fragrance

101. When I Rise, A Meditation

104. Delight

105. Success

107. Uncommon Reasons for Joy

110. Grace

111. How to Listen to God

114. Greatness

115. How to get Closer to God

118. Growing In Faith

122. When Life Gives You a Raw Deal

123. Fighting Fear

125. King of Mercy

127. Your Family

130. What Did You Say?

131. Passion

133. Purity

136. The Ultimate Gift

138. My Child

139. I Am Resurrection

142. Hunger

144. After

145. Song of Truth

147. Secrets of My House

150. How To Simplify Your Life

151. Closing The Gates of Hell

154. The Warning

155. I Want

158. Warrior

160. A Valentine From Almighty God

162. Rebuilding Courage In Your Life

163. Praise to the Lamb

166. Intimacy

168. Come, Holy Spirit

169. A New Champion

171. The Spirit of Offense

The Lion in the Wheelchair

I am a lion in a wheelchair. I will be undefeated because my great Daddy is pushing me. My job is to make the other cats grow into lions. If I teach people to fight, I have to fight myself.

I love the truth and press on to victory. It takes a lot of love to make kittens into lions. I roar and growl, and some people don't understand me. But my Daddy and my infirmities push me on past the finish line.

Then, in an instant, I will be changed into more than I want to be, and so will they, if they believe.

'I will be
undefeated…"

2

"Will you pray with me?"

Dear Father,

We pray that we would not be left alone like broken vines but that we would be knitted together in love.

Help us to cast away bitterness and anger that separate us from you and from each other.

Bind us together as a family so that we can show the greatness and the beauty of the Lord.

Give us tender hearts. Melt our hearts of stone toward the weak.

Open our eyes to see You in every person. May we be vines that bear fruit in every season.

May our lives be filled with the care and kindness of the Lord and may our goal be to show His greatness.

Let us love, let us love, let us love.

A Humble Soul

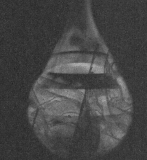

In a humble soul, I asked God why my prayer wasn't answered. He said, "Your mind is too slow to understand me, but I am trying to help you.

There are two key concepts to understand how I answer prayer. ***One is in the fullness of time and second is to reveal My greatest glory.***

The first reason I wait, is to reveal the full extent of my greatness.

Two, is to reveal human weakness.

Three, is to create ongoing community.

Four, is to increase holiness and devotion in the soul.

Five, is that I love hearing your voice.

Six, is that it's not about My answer. It's about My relationship with you. ***My relationship with you is paramount.***

Your cries cleanse your soul and increase your focus. Waiting increases your desire and passion for Me. In this I delight in satisfying your soul.

Sustained By God

Who is there, who can be compared with You, the Son of God, Yahweh our God. You made the mountains to reach out to You. You are Great, Yahweh our God, and Your face, oh God, a Light shining into the darkness.

How glorious is Your name over all the earth. Your love embraces the universe. Who's there that can be compared with You the Son of God, awesome in glory? Every creature comes before You. You are Great. Yes, You are the Lord our God.

When God sings, it's like rushing waters and dancing leaves, sweet kisses and a gentle touch. *When God sings, you pay attention*. Completely captivating, the most beautiful song you have ever heard, except the name of Jesus.

If stars could dance in the sky they would, and waves would roar their approval. All creatures thunder their delight and birds chirp their praises.
The fish dance with joy showing snapshots of praises. If the rocks could cry out, they would.

With every breath He creates a tapestry; always completing to the end.

The finale, I will sing over Yahweh, forever and forever; sweeter to me than the song of a new baby or a loved one.

"When God sings, it's like rushing waters and dancing leaves, sweet kisses and a gentle touch."

8

The Gift

Many of my people are scurrying around, buying gifts. They are afraid of a bare Christmas tree. These gifts are only a shadow of who I am. Why give a shadow when you can give the light?

I am the Light of the World. I am the true everlasting gift. I live inside you. You have become the gift.

You are the light of the world. When you give love, you give light and Me.

My people are craving love, not shadows. Gifts are not bad in and of themselves, but love is better. The true gift is to bring people closer to Me and to reveal who I am. I have placed in everyone a hunger to know who I am.

Will you do your part to bring others there? This is Christmas, it is all about Me. It's not about the shadow, but the light. My light overcomes their darkness.

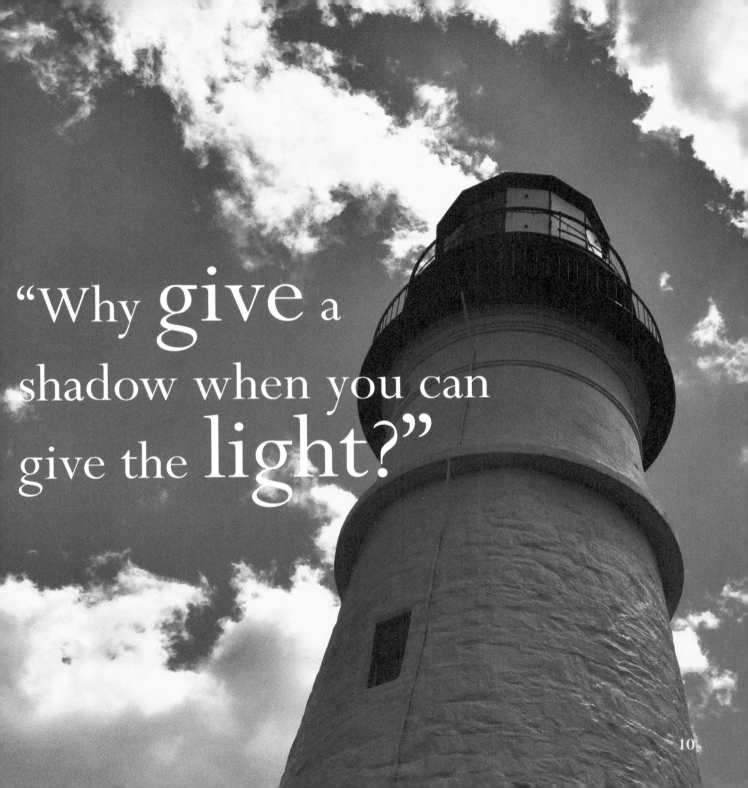

"The devil gladly opened the door."

The House of Self

A man was looking for the house of self. The devil gladly opened the door. Its' address was just me. That is all he was living for. Inside the house were gold and glittering things, which quickly possessed him. The devil laughed and shut the door of the house called self. There was room for just one in the house of self, and no one else was allowed.

His heart grew heavy and his spirit grew dim because there was no one to encourage him. But death came and knocked at the door of the house of self.

You see there was no one else who could live in the house of self. He died clutching his golden things, mourning over what they could bring. There was no one else in the house of self, where love could live no more.

What Will Become of Me?

That is up to you but I, the living God, want to make you a warrior, a champion, a peace maker, a hero. You might laugh at Me and say, "How is that possible?"

I can do anything I want. I am not even going to stop there. I am going to put My glory upon you. You will see My universe in a unique way. You will be richer than the richest man on earth.

You will be a ruler. You will experience My delights and My joys. Your body will be healthy and strong forever. You will have your own mansion paid for completely.

You will meet all my friends and know them forever. You will be eternally without pain and sorrow of any kind. You will eat from the tree of life. You will always have the best of everything. That is what will become of you, My child, My beloved, My precious one.

"You will be richer than the richest man on earth."

Who Am I?

I have been kicked out of homes and churches. I am a teacher, a counselor, a comforter. I help people to be like Jesus but they are afraid of that. They can take only so much of Me.

I am the Holy Spirit. My greatest joy is to delight Abba Father by making His children like Jesus. I am always around but hardly ever invited. Your house is empty without Me. I can fill you with so many good things—wisdom, direction, encouragement and inspiration.

I can change the whole world, but I am waiting… Waiting to be let in your door. I am waiting for the command of the Father to move more forcefully. Without Me, things are dry, empty and more barren. I am life and truth and love. I am waiting at your door to help you.

Humble Man

The humble man approached his Daddy's throne and
prayed for the ones that he loved. Make them mighty
like the eagle, to soar above their circumstances. Give
them the courage of a lion.

Make them like your son, Jesus, and may they never
forget you. Give them the joy of knowing Your
laughter. May their hearts always be innocent and pure
as a newborn baby.

May they all enter Your kingdom and find their places
there. Give them the gift of forgiveness. The humble
man smiled, and was content and thankful.

"Make them mighty like the
eagle, to soar above their
circumstances. Give them the
courage of a lion."

18

"We have a **short time** here, but a long time to think about **how we used it.**"

Time

Time is too short to love, and too long for mourning. Time is too short for thankfulness, and too long for bitterness. Time is too short to let your light shine, and too long to curse the darkness.

Time is too long for yourself and too short for others. Time is too short for giving, and too long for receiving.

God gives us the precious gift of time. We have a short time here, but a long time to think about how we used it.

The Mud Puddle

A man was looking to know God. He found a saint in the mud puddle. "Why are you in the puddle?" Asked the searching man. The saint did not answer the question. Instead, he asked, "Will you jump in my mud puddle?" It smells in here, and you might get stuck. It is uncomfortable and full of pain and sorrow. I have asked many people to help me, but they are afraid to jump in. I have found God in this mud puddle. Will you jump in with me?" The searching man replied, "I would like to help you, but I just don't have the time". The saint waited and prayed, and the searching man walked away, unfulfilled.

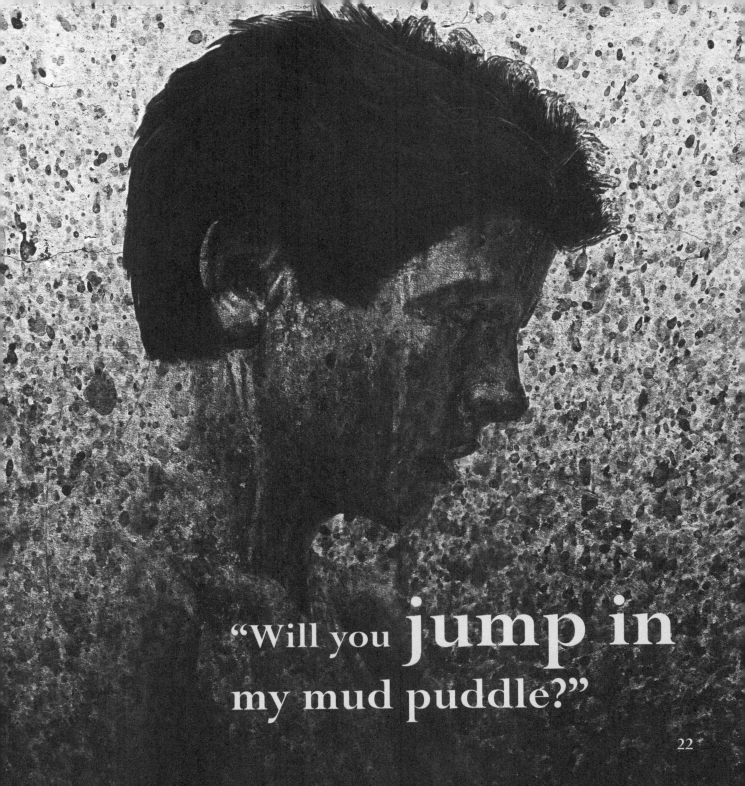

"Will you jump in my mud puddle?"

Friends

Friends are gifts, not possessions.

Friends reflect God's graciousness and kindness.

Friendships have seasons; enjoy them while they are hot, and be patient when they are cold.

A true friend ignores circumstances and embraces the heart.

Friends are treasures found in unlikely places.

We spend more time pursuing our own friendships than friendship with Jesus.

Friendships are not tools of manipulation, but diamonds in the rough.

True friends receive and believe.

If you possess friendships, they will end.

If you share them, they will multiply.

Friendships are like a garden; they require time and work.

Laughter among friends is good medicine.

Sorrow among friends is a healing balm.

Jesus will always be your best friend!

24

Telephone Number & Address

Would you like to have My phone number and address? My phone number is Jesus, and my address is Jesus. Now, did I not make it easy for you?

You cannot pin Me down. I am everywhere I need to be. I do not have an answering service. I always answer every call. You have first priority when you use this address and phone number. You see, I am always waiting for your call and your knock on My door.

It is a very large house, but I always answer right on time. I am busy preparing a place for you here, but I am never too busy for a long or short chat.

My house is very intimate and homey. I cannot wait until you live here!! Just waiting for your call or knock.

With great love,

Jesus

Tenderly

I hold you tenderly and gently, as a mother cherishes her
firstborn child. Your eyes are closed but you will see Me
in My power, My glory and My beauty.

My plans are established for you just as a mother delights
over her child. I will watch over you constantly and
protect you, because without Me you are helpless
and powerless.

Because of Me, you will accomplish eternal things and
have a destiny that will never die. See, my beautiful child,
for your Daddy is bursting with pride! Look, everyone!
Do you not know that I have done a great thing? It is you!
It is you! It is you!

"Your **eyes** are closed
but you **will see**..."

Because of Me

You will outlast the stars in the sky. When the sun is dark, you will be exploding with joy. You will have the beauty of holiness. Your bodies will be powerful, healed and strong.

You will walk with your Daddy in My most pleasant places. You will possess wisdom about My universe. You will be wrapped in and surrounded by My beautiful and delightful music.

You will know the greatest people ever created because you are one of them. Of course, there will be no sorrow or temptation and no evil shall befall you.

You will have the closest intimacy and tenderness with your Daddy God. Your heart will be bursting with joy. It will be continually amazed, astounded and enthralled!

Signed with love,

"You will know the **greatest people** ever created because you are one of them."

"Your bodies will be powerful, *healed* and strong."

Message From The Baby

I am not just a baby anymore, a tiny thing in a crib and straw. I am not an innocent, fragile child. I am a raging lion, ready to destroy my enemies.

I am the Prince of Peace. I am a sovereign ruler ready to take my empire. I am the master creator of all things. I am the Great Physician. I am the tireless warrior. I am the Great Intercessor. I am the wealthiest and most generous person in the universe. I ride My chariot on the winds of the earth.

My footsteps can crush the mountains. I am holy, pure and pristine. No one can match My glorious raiment. My beauty is impeccable and without flaw.

I am yours. I belong to you. I am coming to you, and you belong to Me. I am not just a baby anymore. I am by your side.

32

The Drum

A man came with his drum to worship the King. When his time came, all he could play was rum tum tum, rum tum tum. It was a small and weak song from his tired old drum.

"Why don't you give me splendid songs so that I can be important, rich and famous and You could receive your proper worship?" the man asked. No reply came, but the King beamed with approval delight and pleasure. "You are important, not your drum. I accept your sacrifice." The man was ashamed because he had done such a small worship for the King, but he felt the King's pleasure even more intensely: "Keep going, keep playing. Just come before me as your sacrifice is enough. "

The King repeated his promise to bring him into His heaven.

"the King beamed with approval delight and pleasure."

Focus

Focus is important in my kingdom and in your life. My eyes and heart are always focused on you. You have no idea how intense My affections are for you.

Focus is a necessary ingredient in your spiritual and physical success. Keep your eyes and heart focused on Me and I will give you the focus you need.

There are two kinds of focus you need. The first is focus on Me. The next thing you need to be successful is to focus on the next step that will make you successful.

The enemy likes to distract you. That is how he throws you off course. but focus on Me will give you success. My focus is to use your talents and abilities to build my kingdom and glorify My Son.

Most failures are caused by a lack of focus on goals and details. I will always be there to help sharpen your focus to reach the right goals. So remember, focus on your blessings and not on your problems.

"The enemy likes to distract you."

The Cross

A man carried a heavy cross down a desolate valley. All along the way, he saw a long line of people carrying crosses and seeking heaven.

Along the way, he saw a large pile of discarded crosses. People in this group also asked if they could trade their cross for his.

When the man complied, he found the cross heavier and more burdensome than his own. Others had the same experience, but could not explain why.

At the top of the mountain was a large opening with a huge mirror in the room. There lay a great pile of discarded crosses. Each man who carried his cross saw he had the face of Jesus and heart of Jesus, and continued to walk to heaven.

Since the man no longer had his own cross, he rushed back to pick up his own cross and carry it up the mountain. At the end of his journey, he heard a beautiful voice say, "I have made you like my son. Now enter my kingdom." Your cross is made especially for you.

"I have made you like my Son…"

Watchmen

The watchmen are crying, "Come to Jesus, come to Jesus, and Jesus come down." There are many empty posts. Many watchmen have fallen asleep. They are bound by snakes of selfishness and comfort. Only a few watching, only a few praying.

The enemy rejoices that many posts are empty. There is only silence and the sound of sleeping. Who will hear them? Who will respond? God has placed watchmen on the wall, but many are sleeping. Over the borders, in the mountains and in the plains, they are sleeping. "Snug and secure," they say, "nothing will happen to us." The enemy sees the empty posts and he laughs with delight. He has sent the snakes and they have done their job.

They are sleeping and few are crying. We are so safe and secure. The enemy laughs that we are ripe and ready. Hear the watchmen cry, "Come to Jesus, come to Jesus before it is too late."

Will you stand at your post?

"They are bound by snakes of selfishness and comfort."

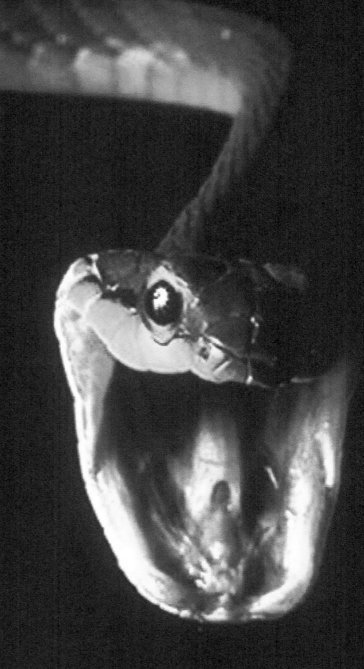

40

"Your goal is not to defeat evil but to celebrate God."

Have You Ever Wrestled With Evil?

Have you ever wrestled with evil? It lurks in your mind so you don't see it. Then it attacks viciously at the opportune time. It constantly tries to convince you that God is your foe. It is defeated by doing countless acts of kindness to others.

You can numb it by songs of praise to God. You shoot it in the heart when you make love your aim. The word of God renders evil helpless.

Your goal is not to defeat evil but to celebrate God. He is the one who will crush your foe. So, keep celebrating and keep trusting.

The Echo

A man went to the Great Throne Room to see what God had to say. It was a simple, " I love you!"

It bounced off the rocks and danced over the waters, it leaped on the mountains and it filled the atmosphere. Everything was saturated with "I love you!" It was completely mighty and infinitely tender.

The "I love you" danced around his heart and filled his being with gratitude. It echoed again and again so he could never forget: "I love you, I love you, I love you!!"

"It **bounced** off the rocks and **danced** over the waters…"

I Was Weak

I was weak. I looked for Jesus. I was in trouble. I
ran for Jesus. I was lost. I took His hand. I was in
pain. I saw His crumbled and crushed body.

I had a victory. I danced with Jesus! I was guilty.
Jesus forgave me. I needed a friend. He was
one. When I was overcome, He held me and
comforted me.

You see, the story goes on and on for you. You
see, the journey is about me, but the story is
about Jesus. It is called history, "His Story".

A Key To My Kingdom

On this day, I will give you a key to My kingdom. It is believing that I am. Do not believe in what I will do for you or false definitions of happiness. You can believe in who I am, My character, My nature, My person. I am a real God, a real person.

I have invested My nature and character inside you, and you can identify with this. My ways may be strange but I am not. I am totally dependable, reliable and trustworthy. What I say is true, and I will do it. You can count on our relationship with your life. That is called love.

This reaches through the corridors of time and into eternity. I am your friend Jesus. I am He who's done amazing things for those who I love. You will see it and you will know it.

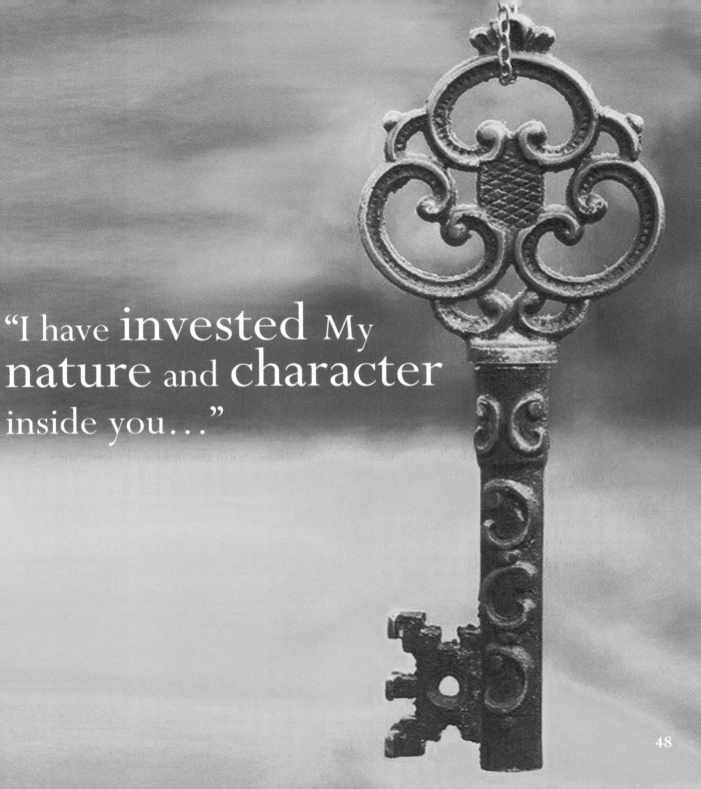

"I have **invested** My **nature** and **character** inside you…"

48

Children, A Parable

Children were playing happily in a pleasant field. They laughed, danced and played together. They cared for each other.

The enemy was jealous and had a plan. He put temptations in the field. One child found a temptation called money. He told no one and kept it to himself. This led him to another one called success. Reputation followed. Care and anxiety about these crept into his soul and occupied his time and attention. He no longer laughed, played or sang. He no longer cared for the others.

The other children also fell to the same temptations. Soon the field was silent; the children were alone but were responsible adults, and proud of it.

Weeds grew in the pleasant field, and the adults stumbled over what they found. They wished they could be children again, who laughed, sang and praised God. They no longer cared for each other. They were alone.

The Meal

I have prepared a meal for my children. It is meat for the mature, and not milk for the young. It is time to stand up for your families, friends and loved ones.

I will provide the just desserts. I will provide the might and weapons of war. Be filled with the Word of God and do not fear. Be filled with worship, not empty phrases. Be filled with words of love and affirmation.

Stand tall; do not run, and fear will run from you. You do not stand alone, but with the Lord Himself. Be wise and resist evil, so that it will not overtake you.

Compromise and indifference are your enemies. They will allow your loved ones to be destroyed. Are you not my hero and my champion?

This hour is made for your victory. Proclaim my salvation! Proclaim my promises! Proclaim my love!

52

Gift of Work

I give you the gift of work. I call it a treasure. My treasure produces
more treasure.

How will you respond to My gift? Will you grumble and complain and waste your
privilege? If you grumble and complain, you will lose your rewards for now and
for eternity.

You can also use this job to give life and help to others. Remember, it's Me that
you are actually serving. I come in many different forms to test your character and
resolve but that only produces more treasure for you.

So love and work and you will be made successful.

The Mask

Did you ever not like it when you saw yourself in the mirror? Don't worry, I have created a person of great beauty. The earth has put its mask on you, full of deception and lies.

If you want to learn to be beautiful, seek Me and follow Me. Look for Me, and you will find Me. In My presence, there is great beauty. You have My presence and My beauty.

The more you know Me, the more it will shine and remove the mask the world has put upon you.

Victory

Hear the hoof beats of victory and the songs of salvation! See the sword of the Spirit raised high in glistening light. Open the great book of God's Word and promises like a mighty hammer will defeat your enemies.

For He has responded to the cries of pain and sorrow from His saints. Rest in this, knowing that He will not forget. Let His mercy and forgiveness cover you each day like a fresh morning dew. May His hand hold you securely and His face shine upon you.

This is your inheritance, which has been assigned to you. Grasp the echoes of joy and laughter that resound through His universe.

Root of Heaven

Why are you dried up, root of Heaven? Have the cares of the world
come like thieves in the night to steal His promises?

The Lord of joy and splendid surprises is dancing and leaping with joy
within you, waiting to water a dry and weary soul.

Open the door! Let Him come out, for the world is desperate for
Him! You are part of the answer, part of His comfort, part of
His revelation.

Will all this not come back to you? Trust in His generosity.

A Tribute

Beautiful , beautiful Jesus who bled and died for me; upon the cross He hung to seal and to save. My champion and my hero who crushed my sin for me; I will see one day in heaven how could it ever be.

Beautiful, beautiful Jesus, your love has made me whole.

Beautiful, beautiful Jesus my heart dances and sings thinking about all the blessings that His suffering brings. My heart dances and sings beautiful, beautiful Jesus.

The Garden

For I have planted within you seeds of greatness, an eternal garden with abundant fruit like My tree of life. It will burst out with praise! It will breathe My name. It will give the fruits of peace, love and joy.

You are not a whim or an experiment, but a masterpiece that reflects a part of Me. Enjoy and give away my fruit. Live in My pleasant garden; it is yours forever. For I have given back what was taken from you.

Go forth in peace and confidence! That is only the beginning of what I have for you; for My face of favor will shine upon you forever.

"My hand has **kept you** from all of this and more."

Rescue

I have rescued you from the eternal fires of hell, from endless loneliness, from the great terrors of the deep, from endless sorrow and pain, from unresolved grief and shame, from endless and continual torture, from unanswered prayers, from separation from My presence, from the end of hope and unrelenting fear, from memory of your mistakes and sins, from unspeakable punishment.

Yes, I have saved you from all of this and more! Are you not glad? Do you not rejoice? Does this make you smile?

One day you will leap for joy at this. Have you forgotten about My mercy? My hand has kept you from all of this, and more.

"Let your **heart** ache."

The Aching Heart

Do you not hear the whispers of praise, the splashes and the glow of glory? Yet our eyes are still not opened. Do you not feel His tender Presence touching you now, filling you with life?

Our hearts are asleep and we do not know these things. Oh that we would see, hear and feel them again. We need them continually, but our hearts seek other things because they are asleep.

Wake up heart! Wake up eyes and ears so that we can see, hear and feel the Almighty Living God! He marches like a mighty man towards us. Let Him come! Let us awake! Let us know all that He is.

So, let your heart ache; it is good for you. It is a privilege to know, see and feel Him. Let your heart ache.

On Target

The only Almighty looked down upon His children who followed the leadership of Jesus. He laughed with pleasure.

He knew their five year plan, their ten year plan and their billion year plan. His to-do list will be completed for each one. There was no error, only perfection. They were right on target, in the center.

The Holy Spirit was providing corrections as needed. Joy was in the house of the Lord while their enemies fell one by one. His people were a complete success, as only He could do.

The fragrance of His presence seeped down into the depths of His children. All errors will be erased, because no sin can be found in the house of the Lord.

See, you can't miss what God has for you, because He is always on target! All His arrows are straight and true.

The Promise

I will reveal and release the secrets of My house, and they shall prevail. They are sufficient and abundant for each time, not by your measure, but by Mine.

If you hold onto your sorrow, you will miss these secrets. I am the provider, I am the enforcer, I sustain. It is I alone. I create continually.

I am doing this for you. Every day will be another blessing for it is My nature to love and provide for you, even abundantly!

The Adversary

The man approached his Daddy's majestic throne to learn how to pray for his adversaries. Then, he heard the Holy Spirit speak to him.

This is what the Holy Spirit said., "Pray I heal others who were wounded because of your thoughts, words and actions."

Then the man asked, "Give me a soft heart towards others who have hurt me. Let me not have a heart of stone. Grant me showers of kindness in unlikely times.

Show me anger and hate are my true adversaries. Give me the grace to pray for favor and success for my adversaries so that I will not be chained to them.

Show me that one day my adversaries will live with me in Heaven forever."

"Give me your soft **heart** towards others who have hurt me…"

Perseverance

Perseverance is a necessary skill in our lives. It helps us to reach our goals. It builds trust and community. We learn to persevere as God pursues us.

True perseverance has a relentless quality. The fruit of perseverance is success in mind, body and spirit. Perseverance produces peace, because we know others can be counted on.

Perseverance tests and strengthens our convictions. Perseverance raises the banner of hope. Perseverance adds destination and focus.

We persevere to reach Heaven and help to bring others there. Perseverance is a gift from God, who relentlessly pursues us until we are His.

I AM

I am Jesus. I fight for you. I stand with you. I pray for you. I yearn and long for you. I know and feel every joy and every pain.

I bring healing and help, and new vision every day, every hour, every minute, every second. This is called complete devotion.

My eyes and heart are totally fixed on you.
You are My treasure and My prize.

Can you see it? Complete attention and utter devotion to you.

I Know How You Feel

I know how you feel about desperation. I felt that way when I hung on the cross and died for you. I called to My Father and He turned His head away.

Desperation is often the beginning of something new. It is a human condition everyone feels. Desperation opens the door to inspiration, where new ideas and approaches to problems begin.

Desperation teaches us to trust because we must. In the middle of this, I am there closer than ever before working out the solution, in My own time and way.

I will be dancing with you.

Desperation forms and shapes you the way I want you to be. When we must let go, it is not easy. When you find desperation, you also find inspiration.

Let Me whisper inspiration to you for I am so near. Desperation and inspiration dance together.

"Desperation **opens** the door to inspiration…"

The Dance of Heaven

The children played merrily around their Daddy's feet, wrapped in the arms of majestic love. He looked down in love and knew each one perfectly, even knowing the hairs on their heads.

He laughed at His plans for them, as He was raising up a mighty army for His enemies. It was right that they first knew the joy of the Lord, before they knew the battles of the Lord.

He wanted each one of them to know His heart, plans and thoughts for the days ahead. His goal was a relationship, because victory was an afterthought to the Almighty.

So, let them play and let them rest at their Father's feet.

Parched

Come, living God, to our dry, parched land! Let Your sweet
mercies fall like rain upon us. Let Your tender kisses be felt on our
faces. Let us be held in Your safe and secure arms once again.

Let our spirits be filled with thanksgiving and praise. Let
us be hungry for all of You. Protect and preserve us
from our enemies, so that we can prosper.

Come, living God! Come, living God! Come, living
God! We are desperate for Your touch. Come and be
with us once again.

*Let us know Your ways and live
them, and feel
Your glory upon us.*

Mighty to Save

I saw an enormous mountain and I could not reach the peak in front of me. The Lord reached down with His strong right arm, because He is mighty to save, and put me at the top.

I saw rolling hills that reached forever and thought they would never end. He reached down with His strong and mighty arm and put me in a pleasant valley. I saw a raging, foaming sea coming towards me, and the Lord reached down and parted the sea with His mighty arm.

He is mighty to save. I think about these times and remember them, because His strong right arm is upon me, and He is mighty to save.

I Need You

I need You more than the dancer with no feet, more than a mother who has lost her child, more than the poor man who has nothing to give, more than the man who gasped for his last breath.

I need You more than the prayer-less nation mocking God, more than a lion that has no roar and cannot run, more than a lost soul waiting to enter the gates of hell. I need You more than a tiny baby without its mother.

I need You more than a giraffe without its neck. I need You more than an elephant without its trunk. I need You more than a man without one blessing to count.

I need You more than an ear that has never heard a sound. I need You more than the blind man who can no longer see his loved ones.

Fill us with Your grace and glory Lord. Open our eyes and ears and let Your Beloved Spirit fall upon us.

Enable us to know Your love for us, and then we will have no need.

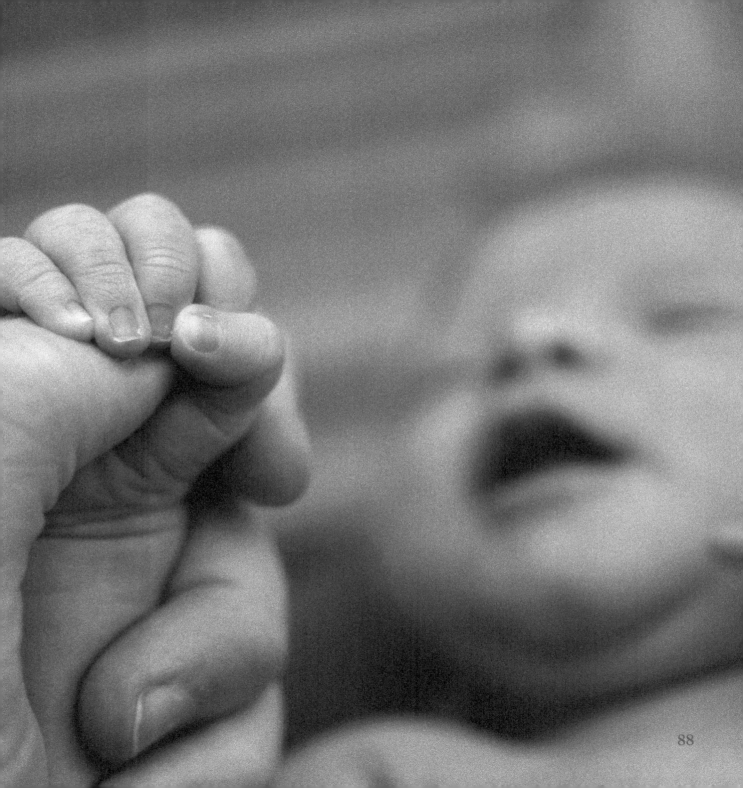

How to Love

This is the season of
Here are some tips
love more effectively.

All love comes from God and Him alone.
It is God who decides whom you will
love. To love, you must give up your
expectations to love the other person.

Let the Holy Spirit highlight whom you are to love;
then study the person's personality and habits. Ask
God for opportunities to serve them.
The giver is more important than the gift.

We love others to worship God, not for our own
purposes. Love is not an act of manipulation. The
Holy Spirit empowers and refreshes those who ask
Him how to love. Let the Holy Spirit inspire you
with thoughts of how to love.

Love is an assignment and a privilege
from God. Pray for the person God
highlights for you to love. Love
to honor God and not to gain for
yourself.

Love is hard work and requires
persistence and courage. Forgiveness
casts away bitterness. Don't give up;
keep trying and you will be rewarded
for your desire to love others.

Keep forgiving yourself for your
mistakes. Love is a tribute to God, and
a memorial to the success of your life.
It's easier said than done.

90

A Fist Full of Blessings

Blessed be the Lord God Almighty! He has poured His loving-kindness over me
like Niagara Falls. He has called me into His family. He has given me a full inheritance of His glory.

I am the apple of His eye, the center of His attention. He is my friend, father and brother throughout all time, and past eternity.

His favor and friendship will never fail me.
He has fashioned my tongue to praise Him. He has given me eyes to behold His love and a heart to carry love to others.

Now, blessed be the Lord God Almighty with every breath I take and with every beat of my heart!!

Humility

Humility turns his face toward God, but pride turns his face toward self. Humility is the basis for knowing, understanding and experiencing God.

God displayed great humility by offering Himself to us. Humility builds community, pride divides it. Humility secures and establishes friendships. Humility makes it possible to approach God.

Humility enables growth and change in us, in our friends and in our enemies. Humility provides a realistic view of life and creates pathways for overcoming obstacles. Humility is the birthplace and guardian of love.

Those who capture humility acquire a divine possession. It is a gift from God. If you have found a humble person, you have found a birthplace for a true friend.

Humility requires work, sacrifice and constant vigilance. Humility is one of God's greatest treasures. ***Humility leads to eternal life.***

Accomplishments

All accomplishments are measured by the love given. Everyone who pursues things will end up with nothing. Everyone who pursues love will end up with everything.

The only true achievement is to love. Everything else is hollow and empty and will be forgotten.

Love has a voice, it will shout God's praises. God knows this truth now and soon we will know this also.

Wrestling

Have you ever wrestled with evil? It lurks in your mind so you don't see it. Then, it attacks viciously at the opportune time. It constantly tries to convince you that God is your foe.

It is defeated by doing countless acts of kindness to others. You can numb it by songs of praise to God. You shoot it in the heart when you make love your aim.

The Word of God renders it helpless. Your goal is not to defeat evil, but to celebrate God. He is the one who will crush your foe. So, keep celebrating and keep trusting!

Sweet Fragrance

I gave you what is left of my body; you have crushed my heart like a rose. May it be a sweet fragrance that reminds others of You.

May it be a sweet spirit that goes on and on. Let my will be like a pounding hammer that drives me closer and closer to all You have for me.

My body, a crushed rose. My spirit, I give it all to You.

When I Rise — A Meditation

When I rise, all the beauty of the universe meets Me, and the glory
of a million suns and rainbows follows Me. My power makes every
wave pound towards the shore; only I can contain it.

If I spoke it, another universe would be created in an instant. When
I rise, all My enemies shake and tremble with tear. When I rise, all
the created jump for joy and dance in unison.
Your wisdom is like a straw in a billion bales of hay, but My
wisdom cannot be contained in everything that I created. I utter
just one word and empires are changed.

It is so. One day I will rise and come to meet you and it will be
finished; you will be left undone. You will weep and shake with joy!

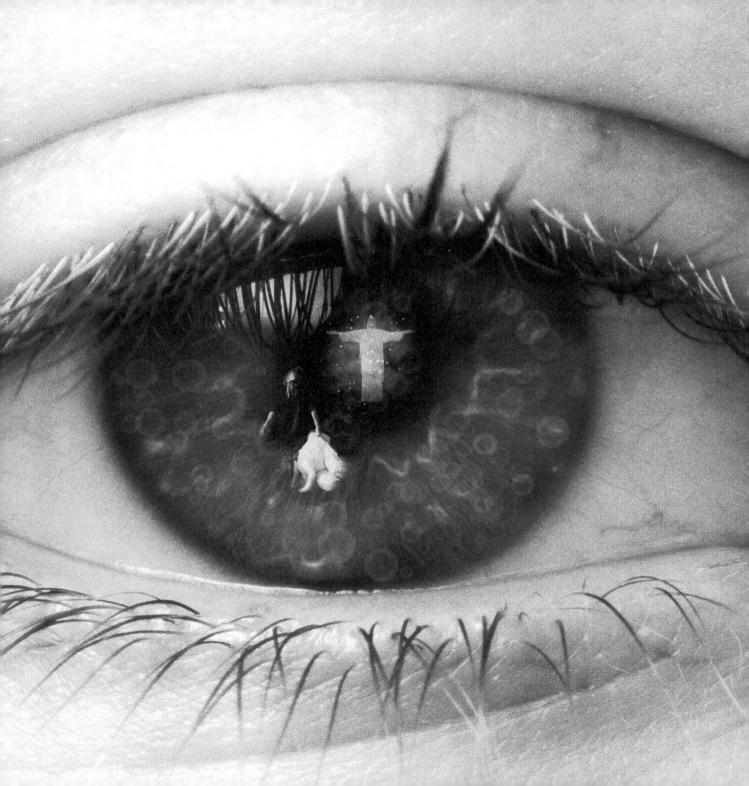

Delight

I have put you together particle by particle, cell by cell. I have poured out talents into you. I have arranged all your true friends.

I have watched jealously over you every second, minute, hour and day of your life. I am delighted by what I have made. It is My joy to bring you home. It is My purpose for you to be reunited with Me. I am delighted in what I have made with you. It is for the glory and praise of my Father alone.

Your beauty and your sacrifice dances before My eyes. How could I forget you? How could I leave you? You are the passion of My purpose. For it is why I was born as a baby, why I died and rose again for you.

It is all about unconditional love and single-minded purpose. You may have failed, but I consider you My success. Because of Me, you will not miss your purpose in life. I am your purpose in life.

You are My delight. Your beauty and sacrifice dances before my eyes.

Success

I have wired you and programmed you for success. Success comes from having a relationship with me and obeying Me. I am success. It is all around Me. It is wrapped in everything I do.

Success does not come from the accumulation of power, wealth or things. It comes from loving Me and others I have placed in your life.

Why chase the ever-changing winds of worldly success? They can never be satisfied. They blacken your soul and empty your heart.

Success is shared with others; it is not an accumulation of your wealth or fame. Your success comes from helping other people be successful. ***Arriving in heaven is the ultimate success story.*** You cannot get better than what I have planned for you.

Simplicity, trust and a child like nature will help you find Me. I have prepared a successful life for you; a successful place. You will not miss it if you trust Me.

I give you success; the enemy gives you failure.

Uncommon Reasons for Joy

God is more persistent than my stubbornness. Even when I can't forget my bad junk, God does. Friends may fail me, but God won't.

God gave me my jokes, and laughs at them. God sees my excellence; I ponder my failures. God delights in my future; I struggle with my future. I feel that I am common; but God finds me fascinating.

God loves me as I am; I do not always do that. God does the work; I get to wait. My joys are brief; his joys are eternal. God will make me good enough because He is so great. My performance is weak, but God gives me a standing ovation.

God runs faster than me and always catches me when I run away. When I play hide and seek with God, He always finds me. God runs every marathon with me from start to finish.

God has an answer for every plan I devise. God wins every wrestling match with me and pins me down. The Holy Spirit loves to comfort me and teach me about Jesus. God helps my friends to stay my friends.

God allows weakness so I can be strong in Him. God helps me even when I get mad at Him. God is smarter than all my clever plans. God is God and I am not. When I freak out, God remains peaceful and precise. God delights in me even when I mock myself.

Grace

By grace we live and move and have our being.
Jesus is the manifestation of God's grace. To
be filled with Jesus is to be filled with grace.

If we want to be like Him, we must be filled
with grace. Without grace, our lives and
society will fall apart. We can do nothing good
or worthwhile without His grace.

We are becoming a rude, crude and graceless
civilization. Grace reveals Christ, promotes
Christ and reveals His intentions and plans.
We struggle with our own efforts because our
hearts are not open to His grace. We should
be needy and often desperate for His grace;
yet, we are desperate for objects, things and
people's affections.

Grace enlightens our darkness and reveals
heaven. Please join with me today in asking
for God's grace upon us. Without this, we are
a mere skeleton and just bones. In grace we
live and move and have our being.

How to Listen to God

Listening to God is both simple and complex, because God is both simple and complex. God is simple in what He does so we can understand Him.

It is hard to listen to God if we don't have a dialogue with God. A dialogue with God means that we have an exchange of emotions and information between God and ourselves. An example is that He gives us His love and His thoughts.

To listen to God, we must develop and guard our relationship with Him. We need to read the Word of God and allow it to be placed in our heart.

We must not only hear the Word of God, but also obey the Word of God. Obeying means that we have a common trust with God that what He says is the best for us.

Prayer is not changing God's mind, but agreeing with what He says to us. Prayer gives life to our soul, mind and body. It is like water in the desert.

Prayer should be a dialogue of love between two lovers. When we love someone, we listen and talk to them. That is what prayer is all about. Try to talk to your spouse or best friend once a week and have a deeper relationship with them; that doesn't work.

Prayer restores our soul and enlightens our mind in a dark and scary world. Prayer is God's hand extended to us. Prayer is tender words to the lover of our soul. Prayer gives us an opportunity to hear what we long to hear. Prayer is the words, "I love you," explained in detail.

Prayer is the look, the touch and the call of our loved one. A voice in the wilderness, water in the desert, comfort to the lonely and afraid, wisdom to the ignorant. Prayer is the seed, the cultivation and the harvest. Prayer routs the enemies of God. When we speak words of love to God in prayer, we can speak words of love to others more effectively. We are then enabled to hear His words of love to us.

Prayer changes weather patterns, changes lives and changes the course of history. Prayer will change your life and your eternity forever.

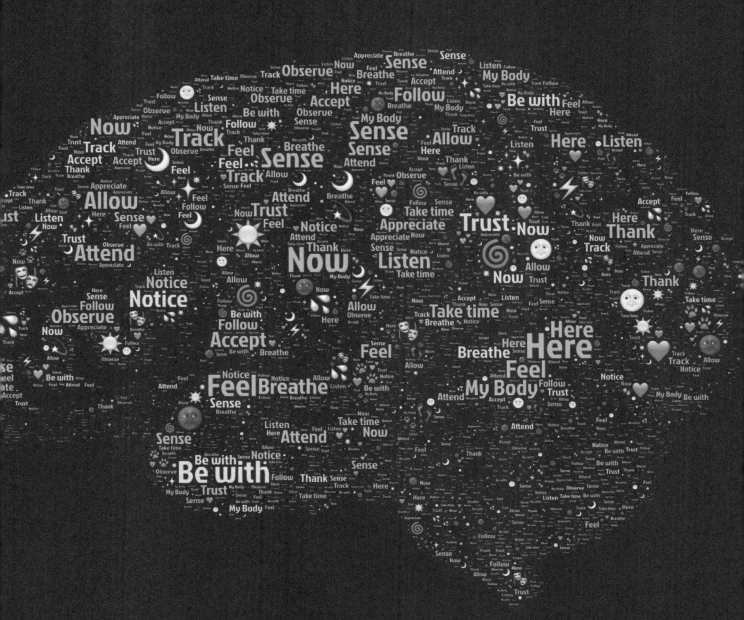

112

Dream

Inspire

Courage

Harmony

Greatness

Greatness does not lie in the accumulation of awards or money. It lies in seizing the heart of God and making it yours. Greatness is a lifestyle to help people reach their best and make their goals.

Greatness takes many forms: humor, inspiration, love, persistence, courage and hope. Greatness is a lifestyle that makes everyone around us better and more beautiful. We prepare for greatness by inspiring others to be great on a daily basis.

Our destiny is to become great because God Himself is great. The ultimate greatness is to be found great in God's eyes because He is the definition of greatness. Loving people is an act of greatness and heroism because so much effort is involved. Loving is the pinnacle of greatness and the most precious possession. No greater gift can be given than the love of a true friend.

Greatness jumps in another's mud puddle. Greatness supports another in his storm. The shrines of greatness are found in the heart of God and in the hearts of your friends and acquaintances.

When you inspire others to be great, they will in turn pass it on. Greatness should be a story retold again and again. You are part of what makes it happen.

How to Get Closer to God

God welcomes us and always wants us to be closer to Him. He loves the humble and resists the proud. Prayer is not to change God's mind but to know His mind.

God resists the grumbler, but He welcomes the worshiper. It's all about God's glory, and not about yours.

Build His kingdom every day, not yours. This is done by helping other people reach their goals or find their dreams. Do little things with great love towards every person. Ask God for the ability to enjoy Him.

God honors others more who love Him and not just serve Him. Your plans are always too little; His plans are always bigger and better.

God honors obedience to Him more than hard work. Receive, receive, receive from Him. We do this by discovering our own poverty and need.
God does not grow tired of giving to you, forgiving you or loving you.

Thank God that you are His prize possession and treat others in the same way.

Cooperating with God

Everybody wants to be on the winning team. God has chosen you to be on His team. God sees you and picks you for His team.

God uses broken, wounded and hurting people to make a championship team. Are you willing to work with Him and others around you? Who has ever heard of an everlasting championship team? God wants you to be on it. Isn't that cool and amazing?

This is not an ordinary championship team, but an amazing one. Collaboration starts with desire, and we need to pray for it. Cooperation continues with sacrifice and bearing one another's burdens on your team. Stars make a difference, so you are a star player in the battle for souls. This is the ultimate game, the one that really counts. Its stakes are high, and rewards are great.

Be ready, for if you do the little things God tells you to do, you will be a star player in the battle for souls. ***It takes only a little to do a lot through the grace of God.***

Growing In Faith

We are all called to walk with the Lord in faith so that we can grow in His intimacy and delights. We are students at faith university until we meet the Lord. In this, God is preparing us for the days ahead, to grow in, spread and share our faith.

God gives us many little assignments to practice every day. Faith is the awareness of our knowledge and use of the love of the Lord for us. In expressing His love, we can also grow in faith. We also grow in faith by prayer, reading and hearing the word of God, and completing the assignments the Lord gives us. They may be small, but they are significant. They are part of a story, His story, that the Lord loves and cherishes. They are the expression of our faithful Father in the power of the Holy Spirit to the glory of Jesus.

We must exercise our faith to grow like a muscle; yes, just a little bit every day will do the job. Daily assignments are our faith therapy where people can see the work of faith in our lives. Those who are faithful in a little will be given much more. Faith is our mighty novel, a beautiful symphony in harmony with God. It will resonate over and over again into eternity.

Faith makes us warriors, servants and lovers. Faith is not just something to do, but something to become. Blessed are those whom the Lord calls faithful to the end.

"Bad things do not come from God, but He uses them."

When Life Gives You A Raw Deal

We all have to deal with this in our lives. We can blame God, or we can grapple with sin. Who holds the universe together? Who named all the stars, one by one? Who knows the exact number of hairs on your head? Who knit you together in your mother's womb? Who made you to live in heaven with Him? Who bled and died for you on the cross? Yes, it was God! God is not punishing you. Only He will give you the best deal possible.

Bad things do not come from God, but He uses them. God reveals His glory by solving your problems. God adds wisdom to your life that you would not otherwise have, and God increases love. We do not grow in love and comfort because we love to stay the same.

God uses our discomfort to cause us to run to Him. God reveals His mercy and His intimate secrets in our trouble. God uses our suffering to give us His nature and character. Are these not good things to have? Satan lies to us and says life is a raw deal, but God's Spirit comes and makes it the best deal for us.

Fighting Fear

Fear will be a major enemy of ours in the days ahead. The enemy will use it as a major weapon to take our eyes off Jesus.

Survival will be the name of the game. The enemy will want us to be increasingly self-centered. Perfect love drives out fear. We need to pray constantly that our love will be perfected and made strong. Fear tries to creep and crawl into the corners of our mind. Fear starts as a little thing and grows into a big thing if left unchecked.

The name of Jesus, the blood of Jesus and the Word of God are the weapons to fight fear. We need to be very aggressive in protecting our house against this enemy. Ninety Nine percent of the things we are afraid of never happen. The enemy's major objective is to cause us to forget about love and center on fear. What the people around us need most is love, not fear.

Centering on the positive closes the cracks in our mind and leaves no room for fear to enter in. Whatever is right, whatever is pure, whatever is noble, we should concentrate on in the days ahead (Philippians 4:8).

"Centering on the **positive** closes the cracks in our mind and leaves no room for fear to enter in."

King of Mercy

It is coming, it is here. Can you believe it? Can you receive it in your heart? Mercy for your coming! Mercy for your going. Mercy for your staying. Mercy for that which has been left undone. Mercy for unforgiveness. Mercy for neglect and unkindness. Mercy for the stains of sin. Mercy for hopelessness and fear.

My mercy pursues the lost and forgotten. My mercy brings life. My mercy is the birthplace of love. Cast away your hearts of stone. Cast away your anger and bitterness.

This is who I am, pouring out mercy upon you. You are a child of mercy, a product of mercy. If you want more mercy, give it away and it will be multiplied back to you.

Mercy makes a way where there is no way. It opens wide blind hearts and blind eyes. Yes, it is raining mercy, mercy and more mercy. Come, I offer you a drink.

"My mercy is the birthplace of love."

Your Family

We were not made to be alone. We are designed for family and community. The enemy's plan is to make us feel alone so that he can destroy us. He uses our selfish desires to keep us separated from others.

Building community requires prayer, sacrifice and devotion, especially small acts of kindness, which knit us together. It is in community and family that we learn about loving one another. It is here that we learn that what is good for others is also good for us.

As we lay down our lives for others, God begins to appear to us. This is because this is what He did for us. We can be alone and be in control, or we can be in family and community, to see the many faces of God. We make a choice every day to build family and community or build walls around us.

Community and family are two of God's best treasures if we are willing to set our hearts on them. The question remains, "What will we set our hearts on?" What we set our hearts on is what will become of us.

"Your words will echo throughout eternity."

What Did You Say?

Good communication has become a lost art in our lost world. Deception abounds because our actions do not match our words. Good lovers are good communicators. The lack of love has left our communication shallow and empty.

We have learned how to speak out of our emotions, but not by the Spirit of God. Bitterness and anger poison the hearts of those we care about.

The foundation of good communication is found in prayer and preparation. The Bible says our speech can bring life and death to another. If we pray and prepare before we speak, our words can be filtered by the Spirit of God. Our words and actions should bring life to those around us.

Worship and praise help to make our words pure and sweet. Every word that we speak will be recorded by the Lord. It will bring about the testimony and history of our life. When we speak, we should remember we are speaking to Jesus Himself.

What would you like to say to Jesus? Your words will echo throughout eternity.

What you speak is what you will become.

Passion

Passion is an idea blown into action. Passion keeps things going and changes the world. Misguided passion is very destructive. Our greatest passion should be Jesus. We can have more than one passion at a time.

Passion happens when we set the affections of our heart on something or someone. Our passion needs a purpose and a goal. When things are in place, good things can happen. Fulfilling passion is a challenge, an adventure, and a journey. When our passions are too widespread, they evaporate.

Passion has two stages: knowing and becoming. We must know it before we can truly become it. We should offer our passions to the Lord, to see if they are truly the ones He gave us. Passions are developed over time and should be tested. The true passion would be to lead us closer to Jesus.

Purity

It is not possible to have an intimate relationship with God by carrying with you a collection of trash and filth. This garbage is a stench to a holy and pristine God. We ask God for mercy, but instead we choose to hold to and do the things that offend Him.

We must first make a choice to cast off the things that offend God and disrupt our relationship with Him. You cannot straddle the fence and have one foot in the world and one foot with God. A prince and a princess do not live in a pigpen.

You are the prince and princess. Purity starts with a series of choices we know will please the Lord. The Holy Spirit will lead us into a lifestyle that builds more purity. The jewel of purity is the possession of what God has and is. It is our way of telling God that we long to have Him and to be like Him.

We were made for love, not rebellion . We will end up with a collection of trash or jewels. Our enemy gives us trash, but God gives us jewels. Why not run after what is best?

Purity leads us to a longer and better quality of life. Purity allows us to feel the fresh and tender kisses of God and their sweet fragrance. What is better than experiencing the sweet and tender kisses of our Creator, and having them into eternity?

"Purity starts with a series of choices…"

i am
grateful

The Ultimate Gift

What is your ultimate gift? Salvation? Love? Children? Life? Liberty? Peace? Money? Joy? Our Lord is the giver of many good gifts. The best way to possess these gifts is to give them away if you can.

Too often we are a grumbling people rather than a thankful people. Gratefulness increases our appreciation for God's many gifts. Boredom and drudgery are the enemies of our gifts.

It might be a good idea to highlight a gift and thank God for it one day at a time. Each gift is designed for a special purpose, time and place. It takes the wisdom of God to use them in the right time and in the right way. For instance, humor may be a gift; but if used wrongly, may not be appreciated.

Gratefulness keeps us from feeling short changed in our life. Let us not be like the man in the parable who buried his talent or gift because it was not appreciated. You were given your gift to bless someone else.

May we be wise stewards of our talents and gifts for the Lord. They may be small or great, but they are just as useful to our Savior. Let us offer them up to the glory and praise of God. Of course, Jesus is the ultimate gift. What will you do with Him?

My child,

You are the apple of My eye, My pride and joy! Inside you I have placed a treasure of joy and delight for Me and My children. Wisdom, strength, courage, insight; The power to change lives. An edge to make the difference, humor to laugh at yourself to get you through the troubled times.

Uniqueness, no one will ever be like you before or again; your smile, your love, your touch, your gifts. You are amazing and you will amaze others. I watch over you every second. I wait and a long for you to speak to Me. I love you so deeply and completely; like no one else forever and forever.

Together, we will be together always. I am waiting just for you!

Love,
Your Heavenly Father

I Am Resurrection

I am alive. Faith calls Me and knows Me. Death trembles
at My name for eternity comes with Me. I dwell with
the homeless and heal the brokenhearted. I care for the
sick and comfort the lonely. I free addicted slaves and the
abused ones from their chains.

I am a friend to the forgotten and hope to the desperate.
I speak for those who can say nothing. I am the treasure
for those who have nothing. I am a banquet for all
who are starving; a fountain for all those who thirst for
righteousness and justice.

I am the heartbeat of My Father. I am the song, the dance
and the joy. I will never be denied or defeated. I will
arise. I will arise again and again from My Father, because
He loves them.

Hunger

I need you my God like the cracked dry earth that reaches its dusty and brittle arms to the coming rain. I need you my God like the hoarse whisper of the singer who is full of song but cannot sing. Yes, like the poet, who is bursting with emotion but has no words to speak.

I hunger to thank You as a parent who sees the birth of their first child. I long to color and draw for You like the artist who is full of pictures, but has no paint. I wait to hear You like the welcome words of a most precious friend. I want to be held by You as one who is most deeply loved. I hunger that somehow You may be pleased with me as a bright eyed child who has given all to his father and then is able to cry out with laughter, joy and pleasure. I need You as the deep roots of a mighty tree that clutches at You for support and takes deep drink from Your waters of life.

I search for You like the restless wind that will nestle into the hand of its creator. I hunger, I hunger, I hunger, I hunger still more. But I thank you and thank you again that one day we will feast together. We will hunger no more for we will be united at last. We will be one!

After

After time I will be there. After dreams I will be there. After defeat and victory I will be there. After love I will be there. After joy and friendship I will be there. After the last song has been sung and the last word spoken, yes, I will be there. When the laughter and cheers are gone I will be there. After rage, terror and fear, yes, I will be there.

When you are all alone and there is no hand left to hold, I will be there. I will be there to make all things new. Joy, laughter and love will abound forever more.

Friendship, progress, success and virtue will be forever more. Faith and victory and peace will be forever more. Beauty, majesty and glory will be forever more. Eternal life is in My hand forever more. I am Jesus. I am forever more.

Song Of Truth

Arise, awake, I am not finished yet. A light is coming; refreshment,
hope and joy, vision, clarity, strength.

No, I am not done yet. I am at work making you more like Me. I am
sending you victory, resurrection; a new power to get things done.

How could I leave you? How could I forsake you? You are my
heartbeat, you are my joy and I shall not leave.

Remember, I can turn things around; I can make all things new. So,
push on and be confident that I am here and I am with you now and
forever, My love.

146

Secrets of My House

I will reveal and release the secrets of My house and they shall prevail. They are sufficient and abundant for each time; not by your measure but by Mine. If you hold onto your sorrow, you will miss these.

I am the Provider, I am the Enforcer, I sustain. It is I alone. I create continually, I am doing this for you. Every day will be another blessing for it is My nature to love and provide for you even abundantly.

"The enemy's plan is
to make things **more**
complicated..."

How To Simplify Your Life

It is not easy to head south by going north. The best way to simplify your life is to run to Jesus. He alone knows all the circumstances and complications of life. He also knows the solutions for every instance. Not to check in with Him is a serious mistake. It will surely complicate your life and add burdens to your shoulders. After we have gone to Jesus and checked with Him, there are other ways to simplify your life. The first is to take a regular time to listen to God for inspiration and direction. Present your problem to the Lord and thank Him for working it out in advance. Define your goals and break them into three smaller steps. Use your energy to move to the next step, and a solution will soon be made clear. Ask a trusted friend or friends to hold you accountable and keep you on course. Let the Holy Spirit lead you to new ideas and solutions for your problem. Practice surrender, and God will move you along towards the solution. He loves to glorify Himself and work on our behalf. Surrender makes this possible. Does not a young child trust his daddy? Tell God you love Him; it strengthens the bond between you two and helps you to hear Him more clearly. Great things grow out of love and trust. Simplicity is a matter of love and trust. The enemy's plan is to make things more complicated; God's plan is to make them simpler.

Closing The Gates Of Hell

As believers in Jesus, we have the authority to close the gates of hell. This is first done by a series of decisions that we can make.

The first question that we need to ask is, "Where will this decision lead me?" We can choose our words and what we see and hear. We close the gates of hell by treasuring Jesus and the Word of God in our hearts.

We close the gates of hell by establishing habits of loving and self sacrifice for others. We close the gates by asking others to pray for us daily. We close the gates of hell by closing selfishness and negative thought patterns before they start.

We can talk about where our society is going, but what we can do starts and ends with us. We close the gates of hell by carefully choosing who are our friends will be, and by living a life of generosity towards others.

You see, there is a lot we can do to close the gates of hell in our lives. We are in a war, and we must be ready to fight for our heart and soul, with the help of the Lord.

"...we must be ready to fight for our heart and soul..."

The Warning

Do you hear the marching armies, the clash of swords and the sound of gunfire? Do you hear their songs of victory? Prepare for war. Put things in order, for trouble can come like a thief in the night.

Keep your eyes on Jesus and hold fast to God. There will be much trouble, confusion and chaos. Things are not what they seem. Be ready, be prayerful. Use your time carefully. Pick your friends wisely.

Hear the cry of the watchmen on the wall. Draw your loved ones close and build relationships with them. They will be a circle of love around you in the days ahead.

"Draw your loved ones close…"

I Want

I want to give to You, to surrender myself, more than the light that fills the sky, more than all the waves that have ever touched the shore. To give to you until my last ounce of strength, until my last breath, to say how much I love you, Jesus. A never-ending story that shouts and sings Your name, like a mighty flood that consumes everything it desires.

I surrender myself to be possessed by You. I give, I lay down, I pour myself out until my last drop has left me. I will share my surrender with all who dare, waiting to be touched, held and loved by You. With pounding heart I give, I surrender, and I am held and loved by You - I am filled with exploding joy!

Warrior

Behold the Warrior comes to free and to save. His eyes are like fire, His hand mighty and swift. His light will pierce the darkness of the fools speaking hollow words and empty promises. The poor and needy will be swept up in great love.

Hearts will be made whole and wounds will be healed. The strong will be weak and the humble strong. Songs of praise will be heard in the streets. Cries of joy will stir hearts. Forgiveness and mercy will fall like sweet rain. Sadness and pain will melt away.

Behold the Warrior will shake governments and nations. Sin and sorrow will take a tumble. For the Great One is coming. Behold the Warrior lives inside you and me.

A Valentine From Almighty God

I am the Lord and I am hopelessly in love with you. Mine is a yearning and aching love; a perfect expression of love, fierce, powerful and passionate.
I am committed to you as My vessel no matter how broken and fragile you are.

I want to give you the most complete joy and contentment that you will ever know. I want to wipe every memory of defeat from you. My single purpose is to be one with you. My ultimate goal is to form you in the likeness of Jesus. My greatest desire is to accomplish My work through you. For you will share in My every treasure, triumph and victory. You will continually celebrate My presence and My joy. There is no end to My love for you, no top, bottom or sides, beginning or end. My love surrounds, engulfs and permeates you. My mercy sweeps over you like the waves of the sea.

My gentleness, tenderness and kindness for you will never run out. My love for you cannot be contained. It will consume all sin and imperfection. I will always give you My best for I take great pleasure in you even as you are now. I will totally annihilate anything that comes against you, for I am the Lord and I love you hopelessly and forever.

Rebuilding Courage in Your Life

Courage is a gift from God. Ask for it daily. It comes from studying and imitating the life of Jesus. He is and always will be the hero and champion of courage.

Courage comes from rejecting negativity and focusing on the good. Courage comes from the fellowship of believers. Courage comes from the inspiration of the Holy Spirit.

Courage comes from repeated obedience to God. Courage comes from facing your small giants in your life and defeating them.

Courage comes from studying and planning to meet the obstacles in your life.

Courage comes through prayer and conversation with God. Courage comes from digesting the Word of God. Courage comes when you realize God believes in you, despite many small failures.

Courage comes when you realize you are destined for success, despite small failures.

"Courage comes from facing your small giants in your life and defeating them."

Praise to the Lamb

Hallelujah! Let the stars dance in joy and the seas lift their arms in praise. Let the waters cast themselves down in worship and reverence.

Let all the sheep of the Lamb gather around Him to marvel at what He has done. He is renewing and reclaiming all that come to Him. The gentleness of the Lamb rolls like the mighty ocean overwhelming all who stand against Him. The love of the Lamb crushes the grip of fear and shrivels the black heart of hate. The mercy of the Lamb will melt the stone soul and embrace the forgotten spirit.

Yes, praise to the Lamb whose words of blessing and judgment will bound and range over all the earth. His triumphant shout will destroy death. His joyful laugh will shake the foundations of the universe with pleasure and merriment.

The food of the Lamb will be a feast to the hungry and the thirsty will drink from the river of everlasting life. Yes, praise to the Lamb who will restore a symphony of phrase that will echo and reecho through all time and space. Together all that is made will exalt Him and will hold Him up in timeless awe.

Yes, praise to the Lamb who lives inside you and me. He made us to be part of Him for all this. The Lamb and you and me.

"Intimacy lives when it is given away yet only lingers when it is received."

Intimacy

Intimacy cannot be demanded for it is a gift. It's roots are selflessness and brokenness for it must be fed by kindness and gentleness. It cannot be held prisoner by circumstances for it cannot be a possessed or it will be crushed.

It is a child of freedom and trust for it celebrates oneness but draws strength from many. Intimacy births joy but grows on the sweet and powerful pain of desire. Intimacy is a dance that comes with halting steps. It's time passes so quickly but it rarely visits quickly enough.

Intimacy is a treasure that must be appreciated, but it too often lies there misunderstood. It has many enemies but is the only true friend. Intimacy rejoices in the moment but constantly hungers for forever.

It lives when it is given away yet only lingers when it is received. Intimacy is a divine glimpse into the heart of God given to the heart of men.

Come, Holy Spirit

Come, Holy Spirit,
and touch me
You are welcome
to comfort or correct me
as you wish.

Make my heart soft to You
and to others;
let it ache for those who do not
know You, let it be home for family
and friends, and a welcome place
for strangers.

Make me an empty vessel
for You to continually rest in.
Pour Your wisdom into me,
so that I may see, know and feel
as You do.

Give me a passionate love for
Jesus; make me just like Him
until you come for me.
Come and touch me, Holy Spirit:
empower me to do
Your work.

A New Champion

A new champion is rising out of the confusion. His name is Jesus, and He will not be bound by the attentions of men.

He is the true and eternal champion. All who really know Him will long to be like Him.

Men offer us trophies, plaques and money, but Jesus offers us eternity for our reward. The champion of this new age will pursue love. He or she will press on despite infirmity, pain, inconvenience, indifference and the lack of love. God Himself will measure these champions by the love that they give despite setbacks.

Being a champion will become an emotional and spiritual accomplishment, rather than a physical accomplishment. The new champion will be honored by God himself. It is God Himself who will provide such a privilege.

It is for us to choose what kind of champion we will be.

The Spirit Of Offense

Romans 14:4 Who are you to judge someone's servant? To his own master he stands or falls. And he will stand, for the Lord is able to make him stand.

A thorn, the pain, the hurt, a proud heart. I was right and they were wrong. The spirit of offense is one of the major weapons of Satan. All of us have experienced this kind of attack. We can vividly remember all of our pity parties and all the times we were neglected, hurt and left out. However, the Lord wants to talk about something very special. He wants to help us to identify this spirit and give us ways to overcome it. The spirit of offense is one of the most neglected and little known works of the evil one because it is such a common experience of mankind. Everyone gets offended at one time or another. It's how we handle the offense that makes the difference. The spirit of offense works very hard at not being seen because to expose him would be to defeat him. Satan likes to wound us with the spirit of offense so that we can dwell on hurt, resentment and pain. One of the ways that you know if you are getting attacked by the spirit of offense is that you dwell on hurt, resentment and pain. Do these thoughts cross your path every day? Is this what your mind dwells on or your spirit mulls over again and again and again; or is it just like a stabbing sword wound that comes every once in awhile and you shove it away. But the end result is that you don't draw close to people like you did before. You stay a little bit farther away. You keep quiet and don't reveal yourself.

"The spirit of offense is crushing you"

The spirit of offense is crushing you. The spirit of offense is smothering you. The spirit of offense is strangling the life out of you. The spirit of offense likes to keep us centered on our circumstances. It says in

Proverbs 6:19, "An offended brother or sister is more unyielding than a fortified city and disputes are like the barred gates of a citadel. An offended brother or sister is more unyielding than a fortified city." That is pretty unyielding. That is how we become when we are attacked repeatedly by the spirit of offense. We are almost afraid to talk to someone for fear that we will offend them or they will offend us. It is that wicked spirit of offense at work in our lives.

The spirit of offense makes our friends isolation, desolation and destruction because if we keep following the spirit of offense, we will end up with isolation, desolation and we will be destroyed. Our lives will be destroyed and our

"Satan likes to take it and twist it..."

friendships will be destroyed. Everything that we hold precious and dear to us will be destroyed because all we will have is ourselves and our own self-centeredness, our pride and our own righteousness. This is how the spirit of offense thrives.

Now Satan works in several ways to accomplish making the spirit of offense as one of our friends. He causes us to be divided when we look at our differences rather than what keeps us together. We say, oh, yes, I am right about my political views. I know how we should react to this situation in a certain way; and as you hear what this brother and that brother did, you say I would never do it that way. How could I ever think this or think that. Not me, Lord. I would not do that. However, the spirit of offense is behind that because we are offended by what other people do or we do not agree. Satan likes to take it and twist it to be a little bit more or a little bit deeper. They do not think like me, Lord, so therefore I am offended or I won't be like them.

The spirit of offense works on us and tells us we need to work on our right to be superior to our brothers and sisters instead of making love our aim. I know what their opinion is but I am right. We silently say in our own hearts and minds I am superior. I know better; I would not do what they do. The spirit of offense is busy at work. The spirit offense is grinding away at us, hounding away at us. The spirit of offense will do anything to keep us from making love our aim. The spirit of offense does not want us to look at anything that draws us together

"The spirit of offense is busy at work"

like the Lord Jesus, our love for one another, our commitment to one another, or the fact that Jesus died for us on the cross. He wants us to look at anything that divides us, not what unifies us.

The spirit of offense places secret expectations in our hearts as if we deserve to be treated in a certain way. The spirit of offense causes us to forget compassion and kindness for the weaknesses of our brothers and sisters. This brother was crude again or he lied again. I would not eat that many pieces of cake. I would not eat that much chocolate, would I; and the spirit of offense is jumping up and down in pleasure and glee because he knows he is accomplishing his purpose. Where is the compassion and the kindness that we need to have for our brothers and our sisters? It is not there when the spirit of offense is there. That is for sure. Yes, we think we have a right to be treated kindly, but often we are among the first ones to think critically of the acts, personality or the past of our brothers and sisters.

We silently, in our minds, judge, criticize, and say I would not be like that. However, the truth is that we are all sinners and we have fallen short of the glory of God. We were slaves to sin and unrighteousness until Jesus freed us from the power of sin and death. As His saints and His people, our only right is to have the righteousness of Jesus. We do not have any other right. We do not have the right to be right or to be better that somebody else. We do not have the right to be unforgiving, to walk in hatred or the right to be angry. I am sorry to tell you that we do not have any rights like that because when we die with Jesus on the cross, Jesus took all our rights away to be selfish and

"We do not have the right to be right…"

self-centered. We do not have any rights to be angry, rude or thoughtless because Jesus took them all upon Himself.

Instead, He wants to give us Himself. As the people of God, we give up our supposed rights (lie from the devil) to become the righteousness of Jesus, to give away the love of Jesus, to proclaim the deeds of Jesus, to fight the battles of Jesus, and to assume the character and nature of Jesus. That is our only right, brothers and sisters. It is not to decide who is better than somebody else, decide who is right or wrong or that our ways are much better. We are not to have a secret judgment in our hearts where we decide that we will not participate or we will not work to agree with our brother and sister. We do not have that right anymore because Jesus took it away. In the history of the world, no one had a right to be more offended than Jesus. But what was His response to His tormentors? No one had more power or authority than Jesus did, yet He let only His love speak for Him. In this world, we will all be tempted to be offended and there is sin and injustice all around; and when a sister or brother offends us, we need to respond in a Christ like manner.

Let us remember that the spirit of offense leads to the kingdom of defense where we look to our own wounds and our own righteousness. In the kingdom of defense, we build a fortress around us, a fortress of defense and righteousness; we refuse to take the righteousness and the power of Christ that He gave us. Would it not be better when we are wronged to think about the wounds of Jesus, the power, and the righteousness

"We need to respond in love…"

of Jesus? We need to respond in love and kindness when we are offended, then the Lord Jesus extends His hands and says, "Here, I offer you love and kindness for your brother or sister, do you take it or do you choose to be offended?" As we choose to be offended, Satan laughs because he knows that as long as we are offended, we cannot be close to God, as God wants us to be.

Let us remember that the spirit of offense is one of the most powerful weapons of the evil one. The spirit of offense poisons our relationships. The spirit of offense keeps us lonely. The spirit of offense makes us afraid. The spirit of offense leaves us cold hearted to God. We say to God, "You didn't do it my way, I'm offended. I don't like that; I'm offended by you, God." As we say this repeatedly, we have a colder heart towards God. The fire of God's love slowly dies, and we become cold hearted, angry, resentful, bitter and we become like the spirit of offense that has attacked us.

Here are some ways to oppose the spirit of offense:

1. Pray for a spirit of gentleness and kindness in our daily lives. We need to pray that when somebody does us wrong, we will not be offended. We can actually pray that, brothers and sisters. He wants us to realize that we are going to be offended, but if we pray for a spirit of kindness and gentleness, God will protect us from the spirit of offense.

2. Pray for a desire to read scripture often and reflect on the goodness of God. The Word of God is like a big hand that

"...pray for the spirit of kindness..."

pushes the spirit of offense away. When we use the Word of God as a sword, it pushes the evil one and the spirit of offense away. When we answer the evil one with scripture and we meditate on scripture, when we think of the goodness of God, it is very hard for us to be offended. It is harder for us to be attacked and dwell on our hurts or pain.

3. We need to pray for purity of heart in our own constant need for God. When was the last time you prayed for a pure heart to know God? When was the last time you prayed for a greater need for God? The cold heartedness, the indifference, the resentment are all calling cards of the spirit of offense because when the spirit of offense is present, he will take us away from God every single time. We need to catch people doing something right rather

than catching them doing something wrong all the time.

4. We need to look at being offended as the enemy. We need to ask ourselves a question, "What good will being offended do to me? Is it helping me do better; am I thinking straighter? The answer to that question is always no. It never helps to be offended but it always helps us consider the wounds of Jesus, the power of Jesus to save us through His love and His kindness. Do we accept the love and kindness of Jesus? Do we hide ourselves in the wounds of Jesus? Do we accept the power and authority of Jesus to rebuke the spirit of offense or do we just become offended and do not fight back?

"...being offended is the enemy "

5. We need to make a decision to love and still be vulnerable as Jesus did for us.

All of us are tempted not to be vulnerable anymore after we are hurt. We say, that is it, I am not going to do it anymore. I am not going to be vulnerable, and when we stop being vulnerable, we open the door to the spirit of offense. The spirit of offense walks right in. What is the description of someone who is not vulnerable? They are lonely, isolated and afraid. They are desolate, destroyed, cold hearted; all the calling cards of the spirit of offense. If we are not vulnerable, and do not keep trying, that is what will happen to us, brothers and sisters. What would have happened if Jesus wasn't vulnerable? What would have happened if He had said 'I'm not going to be vulnerable anymore?'

What would have happened to us if Jesus did not take on our sins or set being vulnerable aside when so many people hurt Him, even His best friends? Thank God for Jesus and what He did for us. Thank God that He didn't take offense; He also wants us not to take offense when somebody hurts us. We can have 100 right reasons in the world to be offended but Jesus says we should not be offended; and that one reason wipes out all the other reasons we have to be offended. Being offended leads us to death, but hiding in the wounds of Jesus and accepting His power and grace to love gives us life.

The Lord says to us, choose life so that you might live. When we choose not to be offended by our brothers and sisters, we choose life. As it says in Proverbs 17:9, "He who covers over an offense, promotes love, but whoever repeats the matter separates close friends." Proverbs 19:11, "A man's wisdom gives him patience. It is to his glory to overlook his offense. What kind of glory do we have? Do we have the glory of our own righteousness which will fade; or do we have the glory of Jesus that overlooks the offense? Do we have the patience of Jesus?

Do you remember how patient God is with us or are we impatient with our brothers and sisters when they hurt us or wrong us? Surely, we will. Surely, I will hurt or offend you and need your forgiveness. Please do not be offended if I hurt you because I need you to love me. I do not need you to be offended. If you are offended, then you shut me out and I end up lonely, afraid, desolated and dead. When you shut me out, then I become offended because when you take on offense, it is easier for others to be offended. Being offended is like a cancer that creeps over the body of Christ,

> *"What kind of glory do we have?"*

and as we kill the spirit of offense, we will be healthier and healthier. However, when we become offended, we become isolated and unable to love. I can't love, I'm too offended. I can't care, I'm too offended. I can't pray, I'm too offended. I am offended at you, God. The spirit of offense leads to death in our spirits, our relationships with our brothers and sisters and our relationship to God. It is so very important that we do not become offended and look to the example of Jesus for us.

As it says in I Thessalonians. 5:13, "Live in peace with each other and we urge you brothers, warn those who are idle. Encourage the timid, help the weak, be patient with everyone. Make sure that no one is paid back wrong for wrong. But always try to be kind to each other and everyone else. Now may God Himself, the God of all peace, sanctify you through and through and may your whole spirit and body be kept blameless at the coming of our Lord Jesus Christ. The one who calls you is faithful and He will do it."

He will do it, brothers and sisters, if you reach out to Him. He will take the spirit of offense from you. He will take away and rob Satan of one of his major weapons to destroy you and His church. Let's love one another, care for one another and choose not to be offended. Let's be a real example of love to one another. That is the call of Jesus as He holds out His wounded hand. Will you accept the thorns of life because the wounds will lead to our redemption?

> *"...choose life so that you may live."*

To be continued...

— Michael Carr